D0116671

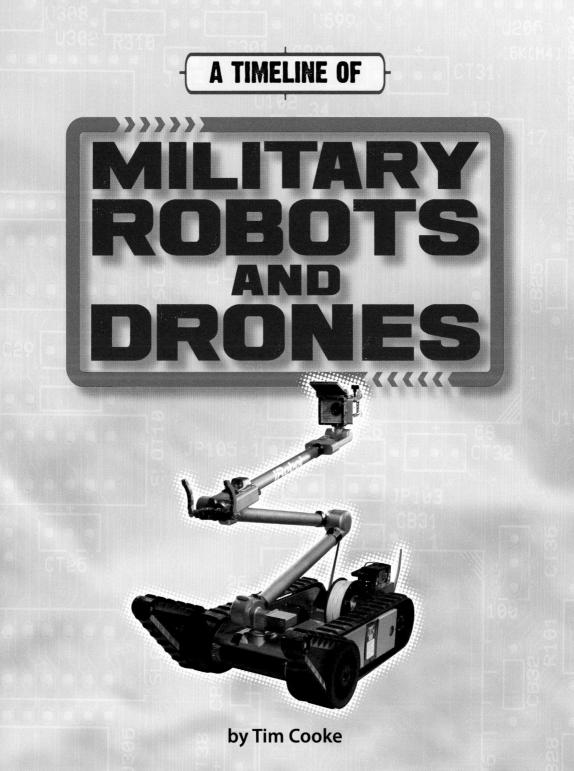

A TIMELINE OF

MILITARY ROBOTS AND DRONES

by Tim Cooke

CAPSTONE PRESS
a capstone imprint

Edge Books are published by Capstone Press,
1710 Roe Crest Drive, North Mankato, Minnesota 56003
www.capstonepub.com

Published in 2018 by Capstone Publishing Ltd

Library of Congress Cataloging-in-Publication Data
Cataloging-in-publication information is on file with the Library of Congress.

ISBN: 978-1-5157-9199-7 (library binding)
ISBN: 987-1-5157-9205-5 (eBook PDF)

For Brown Bear Books Ltd:
Managing Editor: Tim Cooke
Designer: John Woolford
Editorial Director: Lindsey Lowe
Design Manager: Keith Davis
Children's Publisher: Anne O'Daly
Picture Manager: Sophie Mortimer
Production Director: Alastair Gourlay

Photo Credits
Front Cover: Baku13: tc; Department of Defense: cl, bc; iRobot: cr.
Interior: Aerosonde Ltd.: 18br; Airbus Space and Defence: 23bc; Alamy: Chronicle 4; BAE Systems: 25bc; Baku13:
6-7; Base Borden Military Museum: 23tr; Department of Defense: 8-9, 10-11, 11bc, 12-13, 12bc, 15tr, 15bc, 16-17,
16br, 18-19, 19tr, 19br, 20bc, 21bl, 26-27, 26br, 27tr, 27br, 28-29, 29tr; Digger DTR: 22-23; Getty Images: Frederick
M. Brown 17cr; iRobot: 1, 20-21, 21tr; Jjamwal: 24bc; Lockheed Martin: 29br; MineWolf: 22br; NASA: 17bc; National
Archives: 11tr, 13tr, 13bc; National Nuclear Security Administration: 10bc; Prox Dynamics: 24-25, 25tr; QuinetiQ
North America: 28br; Raytheon: 14-15; Robert Hunt Library:5tr, 5cr, 5bl, 6br, 7tr, 7bc, 8br, 9tr; Shutterstock: Everett
Historical 9bc; United Kingdom Ministry of Defence: 14bc.

Brown Bear Books has made every attempt to contact the copyright holders.
If you have any information please contact licensing@brownbearbooks.co.uk

Printed in the USA
5607/AG/17

TABLE OF CONTENTS

MACHINES OF WAR

All armies want to avoid **casualties** in war. Soldiers who are killed or wounded are difficult to replace. From early times military commanders have used ways to attack the enemy that do not put soldiers or sailors at risk. About 2,500 years ago, Greek soldiers from Athens fought a naval battle against the city of Syracuse. The Syracusans set fire to an old ship. They let it drift among the Athenian ships, setting fire to them. Navies used fireships for hundreds of years. They were useful weapons. The ships were impossible to steer, however.

In the early 1900s engineers learned to control weapons using radio signals. Since World War II (1939–1945), scientists have developed unmanned aerial vehicles (UAVs), usually known as drones. Scientists have also invented other types of robots, or machines, that can carry out dangerous tasks on the battlefield.

BALLOON ATTACK

In 1849 the people of Venice rebelled against the Austrians who had governed the city since 1797. On August 22 the Austrians launched some 50 unmanned hot-air balloons carrying explosives toward Venice. The balloons had **fuses** timed to blow up after 30 minutes. They caused little damage to their targets.

AUTOMATIC PLANES

During World War I (1914–1918), U.S. inventors Elmer and Lawrence Sperry had the idea of a pilotless flying bomb. They built a device that became known as the Hewitt-Sperry Automatic Airplane. The craft was steered by remote control and had automatic stabilizers. The war ended before the device could be used.

REMOTE CONTROL

In 1898 inventor Nikola Tesla demonstrated a remote-controlled boat in New York. Tesla steered a model boat using radio signals. Military engineers soon began experimenting with full-size remote-control weapons.

GERMAN FL-BOAT

During World War II, German engineers used a remote-controlled boat. The Fernlenkboot, or FL-boat, carried explosives. It was steered by electrical signals sent along a long wire from the shore. The operator steered the FL-boat close to enemy ships, then blew it up.

casualty—a person who is injured or killed in a war
fuse—a timer that controls when a bomb explodes

TRACKED BOMBS

In World War II the Germans developed a number of uncrewed vehicles. One was an updated version of the FL-boat. Others were for use on land.

The Goliath was a remote-controlled explosive mini-tank. It was steered by an operator using a joystick. The vehicle carried up to 220 pounds (100 kilograms) of explosives. The operator steered it close to buildings or bridges. When it was in position, the operator blew it up. The Goliath was powerful, but it could only be used once, which made it an expensive weapon.

CATERPILLAR TRACKS helped Goliath travel over uneven ground.

REAR OF VEHICLE was attached to an electrical control cable.

TIMELINE

1932
FAIREY QUEEN
The British Royal Navy adapts Fairey airplanes to fly without pilots. It uses these Fairey Queen drones for target practice for naval gunners.

1939
TELETANK
The Soviet Union introduces a full-size remote-controlled vehicle, the Teletank. The weapon is used in the Russian war against Finland.

SPECIFICATIONS

GOLIATH

Weight: 820 pounds
(370 kilograms)
Length: 4 feet 9 inches
(1.5 meters)
Main armament:
220 pounds (100 kilograms)
of explosives
Range: 0.93 mile
(1.5 kilometers)

IN ACTION

GOLIATH

German **combat engineers** used Goliath to demolish walls and bridges. The mini-tanks were useful in urban settings, such as Warsaw in Poland. The Germans used the bombs against positions held by the Polish **resistance**. However, Goliath's armor was quite thin. The vehicles could be destroyed by enemy anti-tank missiles.

ARMOR
was only 2 inches
(5 mm) thick. It did
not provide
reliable protection.

1940

OQ-2 RADIOPLANE
The U.S. Radioplane Company manufactures the OQ-2 target drone. It is the first mass-produced drone in the world.

1942

GOLIATH
German combat engineers begin using Goliath, a tracked mine controlled remotely.

combat engineer—a soldier who performs demolitions or does construction work
resistance—a secret organization resisting a foreign army

UNMANNED AIRCRAFT

The German Air Force was called the Luftwaffe. Its pilots found it difficult to hit enemy ships at sea. German scientists came up with a bomb that could be steered to hit its target.

The bomb was called the Fritz X. It was radio controlled by a **bombardier** in the airplane that dropped it. As the bomb fell toward the sea, the bombardier used a control to move flaps on the bomb's tailfin. As the flaps opened or closed, they changed the bomb's direction. The Fritz X was the world's first precision guided bomb. It grew less effective when the British figured out how to block the radio signals between the bomb and the airplane.

TAILFIN
had movable flaps to steer the bomb as it fell to its target.

WINGS
kept the bomb stable and prevented it tumbling as it fell.

TIMELINE

1942
TD2D-1 KATYDID
The U.S. Navy begins using the McDonnell TD2D-1 as a target drone for anti-aircraft practice.

1943
FRITZ X
German pilots begin using the Fritz X guided bomb to destroy cargo ships in the Atlantic Ocean.

SPECIFICATIONS

FRITZ X
Weight: 3,000 pounds
(1,362 kilograms)
Length: 11 feet (3.32 meters)
Main armament: 705-pound
(320-kilogram) explosive **warhead**
Range: 3.1 miles (5 kilometers)
Top speed: 770 miles
(1,235 kilometers) per hour

POWER PEOPLE

WARHEAD
at the front of the bomb could pierce armor on enemy ships.

UAV PIONEER

Reginald Denny was a well-known Hollywood actor in the early to mid 1900s. He was a pilot in World War I and became a stunt pilot. Denny was fascinated by remote-controlled airplanes. In the 1930s he founded a company to develop UAVs. In 1940 the U.S. Army began to use Denny's OQ-2 Radioplane as a target drone. Gunners used the drone to practice firing their weapons.

5260 AO

1943

FLYING BOMB

The Germans launch V-1 flying bombs toward London. The engines on the aircraft cut out after a set time, and the bomb falls toward its target.

1943

HENSCHEL Hs 293

The Germans introduce a guided anti-ship missile named the Henschel Hs 293. The missile is powered by its own rocket engine.

bombardier—the member of an airplane crew who aims and releases bombs
warhead—the part of a bomb or missile that carries explosives

TARGET DRONES

FIREBEE
is launched from
the wings of a
DC-130 Hercules.

After World War II, the United States competed for international influence with the Soviet Union. The conflict is known as the Cold War (1947–1991). Both sides built up stocks of weapons.

Each country developed jet fighter planes armed with missiles. The United States developed a series of target drones to test the new weapons. Drones such as the Ryan Firebee were launched from airplanes to act as targets for the missiles. The missiles carried **sensors** that detected heat released by the engines of the drones. The missiles turned to follow the heat. At the end of the exercise, the drones were collected so that they could be reused. As the drones fell suspended from **parachutes**, a helicopter used a net to catch them. If the Firebee fell in water, it floated until it was retrieved.

OUTLET
releases exhaust gas
from the jet engine
in the drone to push
the drone through
the air.

TIMELINE

1946
BIKINI ATOLL
U.S. B-17 bombers are adapted to be steered by radio control. They fly above Bikini Atoll in the South Pacific to take photographs of atomic bomb tests.

1946
KDG SNIPE DRONE
The U.S. Navy introduces a small target drone, the KDG Snipe. It was launched by catapult. At the end of a mission, it fell to Earth on a parachute.

SPECIFICATIONS

RYAN FIREBEE

Weight: 1,500 pounds
(680 kilograms)

Length: 21 feet 11 inches
(6.68 meters)

Main armament: None

Top speed: 690 miles
(1,110 kilometers) per hour

Range: 796 miles
(1,281 kilometers)

VIETNAM WAR

During the Vietnam War (1955–1975), U.S. forces used the Ryan Firebee as the basis for a new drone. This UAV was known as the Ryan Model 147A Fire Fly. The Fire Flies carried cameras. They took photographs as they flew above Vietnam. Military analysts studied the images for evidence of enemy activity. The photographs helped them to locate North Vietnamese weapons, such as camouflaged anti-aircraft bases (above).

FINS
at the back of the drone keep it stable in flight.

1955

RYAN FIREBEE
The Ryan Firebee becomes the first jet-powered drone.

1956

AQM-35 DRONE
U.S. forces introduce the AQM-35 target drone. It flies faster than the speed of sound, 676 miles (1,235 km) per hour.

sensor—a device that measures and responds to heat, noise, or other forms of energy
parachute—a cloth canopy that slows down objects or people as they fall through the air

RECONNAISSANCE

During the Cold War, the United States used high-altitude spy planes. When the Soviets shot down a spy plane, U.S. scientists experimented with uncrewed spy planes.

The Lockheed D-21 was designed to be launched from another airplane. It flew at very high **altitude**, close to the edge of space. Its streamlined shape allowed it to fly at three times the speed of sound. The drone took photographs. It dropped the film in a container to be picked up by another airplane. The drone then self-destructed. The D-21 flew four missions over China. Two crashed, and the film from the other two was lost. The program was canceled in 1971.

INTAKE
for jet engine powered the drone.

D-SHAPED
delta wings are streamlined for maximum speed.

TIMELINE

1960
SHOT DOWN
A U.S. spy plane flown by pilot Gary Powers is shot down over the Soviet Union. The U.S. develop uncrewed **reconnaissance** drones in response.

1964
WAR IN VIETNAM
U.S. ships clash with North Vietnamese forces. U.S. drones fly over China. They check for signs that China is arming itself to help the North Vietnamese.

SPECIFICATIONS

LOCKHEED D-21
Weight: 11,000 pounds
(5,000 kilograms)
Length: 42 feet 10 inches
(12.8 meters)
Main armament: None
Top speed: 2,210 miles
(3,560 kilometers) per hour
Range: 3,450 miles
(5,550 kilometers)

UPRIGHT FIN
keeps drone level
as it flies.

IN ACTION

MRBM LAUNCH SITE 1
SAN CRISTOBAL, CUBA
23 OCTOBER 1962

CRISIS IN CUBA

In 1962 U.S. spy aircraft
and reconnaissance
drones photographed air
bases on Cuba. Analysts
could see missiles there.
They were Soviet missiles,
aimed at the United States.
The U.S. government
ordered the Russians
to remove the weapons.
U.S. ships prevented
Russian ships from sailing
to Cuba. For 13 days,
people believed a nuclear
war might start. In the end,
the Russians removed the
missiles from Cuba.

1964 ▶▶▶

RYAN FIREFLY
The Ryan Firefly becomes
the main U.S. drone for
reconnaissance in
Vietnam. It is updated
several times during
the war.

1964 ▶▶▶

VIETNAM
U.S. commanders set
up a special base for
drone operations at
Bien Hoa Air Base in
South Vietnam.

altitude—height above sea level
reconnaissance—military observation to find out information about the enemy

WEAPONS SYSTEMS

Soldiers operating weapons are often exposed to enemy fire. In the 1980s naval commanders introduced robotic weapons that can be fired remotely.

Remote-controlled weapons include weapons mounted to the roofs of armored vehicles. The weapons units contain guns and grenade launchers that are fired by a gunner from inside the vehicle. At sea, the U.S. Navy uses the Phalanx Close-In Weapons System (CIWS). The Phalanx has a cannon linked to a **radar** system. The system detects enemy missiles approaching the ship. Without any input from an operator, the weapon tracks the missile. It figures out automatically when to fire in order to destroy the missile.

> **RADAR** detects and tracks incoming missiles.

> **GUN** has six revolving barrels for maximum speed of fire.

TIMELINE

1972

WHEELBARROW
The British Army uses a tracked vehicle to disarm terrorist bombs in Northern Ireland. The remote-controlled device is nicknamed the Wheelbarrow.

1973

YOM KIPPUR WAR
Israel launches drones to confuse anti-aircraft gunners in a war against neighboring Syria and Egypt.

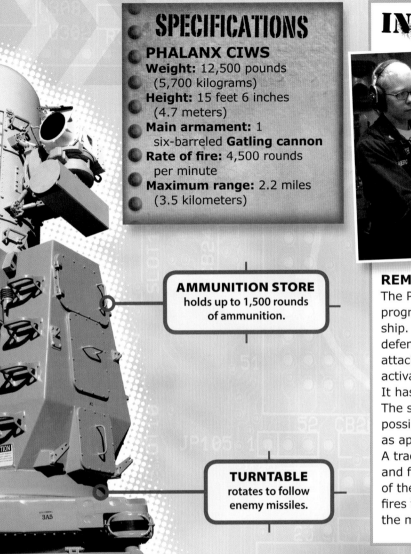

INSIDE OUT

AMMUNITION STORE
holds up to 1,500 rounds
of ammunition.

TURNTABLE
rotates to follow
enemy missiles.

REMOTE CONTROL

The Phalanx CIWS is
programmed on board a
ship. It is activated as a last
defense if the ship is under
attack. Once the CIWS is
activated, it controls itself.
It has two radar systems.
The search system identifies
possible threats, such
as approaching missiles.
A tracker radar takes over
and figures out the course
of the missile. The Phalanx
fires the cannon to destroy
the missile in the air.

1980 ≫≫

SEA-WHIZ
The U.S. Navy fits
the Phalanx CIWS
to naval ships.

1982 ≫≫

DEFEAT OF SYRIA
Israel uses drones to
disable Syrian anti-aircraft
weapons during an Israeli
invasion of Lebanon.

radar—a location device that works by bouncing radio waves off objects
Gatling cannon—a machine gun with a number of rotating barrels

MODERN DRONES

The first modern unmanned aerial vehicles, or drones, appeared in the 1990s. At first they were used for observation. Later they were armed with missiles.

The U.S. Air Force used drones for reconnaissance in the Gulf War (1991). Pilots on air bases in the United States used remote controls to fly drones above Iraq. **Satellite** technology showed the pilots the landscape on the ground. In the mid-1990s the Air Force started using the Predator drone. After 2001, the Predator was armed. It carried air-to-ground missiles. The Predator became the main weapon used to strike against terrorists in wars in Afghanistan and Iraq.

DOME at the front carries electronic systems that allow the drone to be flown remotely.

TURRET at the front carries two 360-degree cameras. One records video, the other detects **infrared** energy.

TIMELINE

1984
AMBER PROGRAM
Engineer Abraham Karem develops the Amber drone. It could be used for reconnaissance or could be converted into an armed missile.

1991
RQ-2 PIONEER
In the Gulf War, U.S. drones observe Iraqi bases. Some soldiers surrender to a U.S. drone by raising their hands as it flies overhead.

SPECIFICATIONS

MQ-1 PREDATOR

Weight: 1,130 pounds (512 kilograms)

Length: 27 feet (8.22 meters)

Main armament: Up to 4 air-to-air or 6 air-to-ground missiles

Top speed: 135 miles (217 kilometers) per hour

Range: 675 miles (1,100 kilometers)

POWER PEOPLE

ABRAHAM KAREM

Israeli engineer Abraham Karem (born 1937) built his first drone during the Yom Kippur War (1973). In the 1970s he moved to the United States and set up a drone development program. He invented the Amber drone, which later became the Predator.

HELLFIRE missiles are carried on two **hardpoints** beneath the wings.

1993 ⟩⟩⟩

GNAT 750

U.S. forces begin to use the Gnat 750 as an observation drone.

1994 ⟩⟩⟩

PREDATOR

The Predator MQ-1 makes its first flight. It is a variation of the Amber and Gnat drones.

---

satellite—communications based on devices in orbit in space around the Earth

infrared—an invisible form of energy, such as heat

hardpoint—a place on an airplane designed to carry weapons

THE WAR ON TERROR

Beginning in 2001 U.S. forces fought terrorists and rebels in Afghanistan and Iraq. The U.S. military developed a range of new drones to perform different tasks.

WINGSPAN
of 131 feet (39.9 meters) helps the RQ-4 fly at heights of up to 60,000 feet (18.3 kilometers).

The main task was reconnaissance. A drone such as the RQ-4 Global Hawk could stay in flight for hours. It had cameras that showed everything that happened on the ground. Analysts watching the images on screens in the United States identified terrorist bases. They even identified individual terrorists. Once a target had been identified, U.S. commanders could send in special forces to attack it. Or they could use drones to launch missiles at terrorist or **insurgent** targets.

HIGH RESOLUTION
camera means images are high quality even at high altitudes.

TIMELINE

1995

PREDATOR
U.S. forces use the Predator drone for observation during the Yugoslav Wars (1991–2001) between ethnic groups in the former Yugoslavia.

1998

AAI AEROSONDE
An Australian drone named the Aerosonde makes the first flight across the Atlantic Ocean.

RQ-4 GLOBAL HAWK

- **Weight:** 14,950 pounds (6,781 kilograms)
- **Length:** 47 feet 8 inches (14.5 meters)
- **Main armament:** None
- **Top speed:** 391 miles (629 kilometers) per hour
- **Range:** 14,154 miles (22, 779 kilometers)

U.S. AIR FORCE

TURBOFAN ENGINE is able to fly for 32 hours without refueling.

EYEWITNESS

❝ As it was summer, we were sitting on the roof of the hospital because it was so hot. We heard a buzzing noise. At the time people never knew that buzzing was a drone. Later we became used to it. There was some noise then from the east, a flash of light came. There was a big blast. ❞

A Pakistani medical worker describes the first U.S. drone strike on Pakistan, 2004

1998

RQ-4 GLOBAL HAWK
The RQ-4 Global Hawk enters service as a long-range, high-altitude reconnaissance drone.

2001

ARMED PREDATOR
U.S. Predator drones are armed with Hellfire missiles. The missiles are used for precise strikes against enemy positions and individuals.

insurgent—a person fighting against a government

BOMB DISPOSAL

In Afghanistan and Iraq, insurgents plant bombs beside roads. Many bomb disposal experts have died trying to defuse these bombs. Now robots make the task far safer.

The bombs are called **improvised** explosive devices (IEDs). They have killed many U.S. soldiers and their **allies**. Modern U.S. combat engineers use a remote-controlled robot called Packbot. A laptop computer steers PackBot next to a suspected bomb. The camera on the robot allows the combat engineers to study the device. Then they use the robot's mechanical arm to disarm the bomb. The arm is very flexible, so it can dismantle most devices. If a bomb does blow up, the PakBot is very strong. It does not get badly damaged — and no soldiers are hurt.

CAMERA
shows the remote operator exactly where the robot is.

FLIPPERS
allow PackBot to right itself if it overturns.

TIMELINE

2002
RQ-7 SHADOW
U.S. forces begin using the small RQ-7 drone. It is launched from a mobile launcher. The drone sends video footage to troops on the ground below.

2003
DECOY TARGETS
In Iraq, U.S. drones act as targets for Iraqi air defenses. When the hidden Iraqi units open fire, U.S. aircraft locate and destroy them.

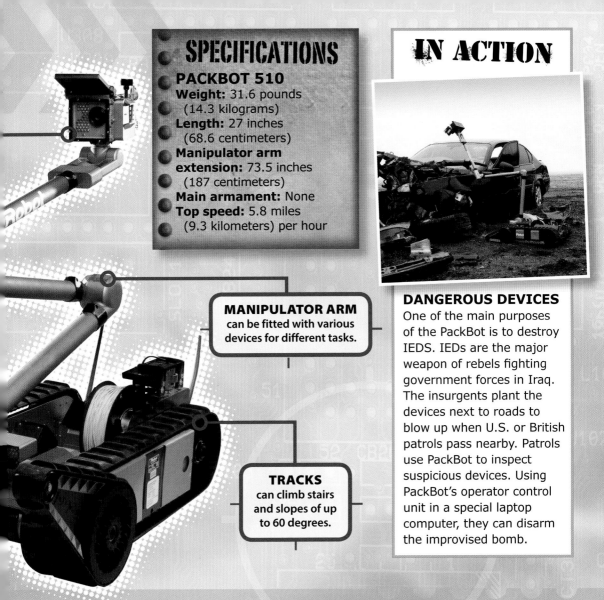

SPECIFICATIONS

PACKBOT 510

Weight: 31.6 pounds
   (14.3 kilograms)
Length: 27 inches
   (68.6 centimeters)
**Manipulator arm
extension:** 73.5 inches
   (187 centimeters)
Main armament: None
Top speed: 5.8 miles
   (9.3 kilometers) per hour

IN ACTION

MANIPULATOR ARM
can be fitted with various
devices for different tasks.

TRACKS
can climb stairs
and slopes of up
to 60 degrees.

DANGEROUS DEVICES

One of the main purposes of the PackBot is to destroy IEDS. IEDs are the major weapon of rebels fighting government forces in Iraq. The insurgents plant the devices next to roads to blow up when U.S. or British patrols pass nearby. Patrols use PackBot to inspect suspicious devices. Using PackBot's operator control unit in a special laptop computer, they can disarm the improvised bomb.

2003 ▶▶▶

RQ-11 RAVEN

U.S. forces begin using the RQ-11 drone. It can be carried in a backpack and thrown into the air.

2007 ▶▶▶

510 PACKBOT

PackBots in Iraq have sound sensors. The sensors help the robots track rifle fire in order to identify the hiding places of snipers.

improvise—to create without special planning or equipment
ally—a group or country that works together with other groups or countries
      to achieve a purpose

MINE CLEARANCE

Mines are buried bombs. They are invisible from above the ground. Mines blow up when a person or vehicle puts pressure on them. They cause death and can leave people with devastating injuries.

As long ago as World War I, armies used armored tanks to clear minefields. The tanks spun blunt chisels or heavy chains called flails that detonated the mines. Modern armies use small remote-controlled robots to do the same job. The Digger D-3 has spinning chisels or chains at the front. The blades blow up any mines as they pass. The Digger is protected by a large steel bucket. Caterpillar tracks mean that the Digger can operate even on rough, uneven ground.

BUCKET ARM
can be lifted to operate at the front or rear of vehicle.

STEEL CATERPILLAR TRACKS
operate on uneven ground.

TIMELINE

2007

MQ-9 REAPER
U.S. forces introduce the MQ-9 Reaper. It is designed as a **hunter-killer** drone. It carries bombs and missiles to strike targets on the ground.

2008

MINEWOLF
A mini version of the Minewolf used by British and German armed forces is developed for mine clearance.

SPECIFICATIONS

DIGGER D-3
Weight: 7.9 tons
(7.22 metric tons)
Length: 18.8 feet (5.73 meters)
Speed: 1.25 miles (2 kilometers)
per hour
Chains: 26
Rotation speed: Up to 800
rotations per minute
Range: 1,640 feet (500 meters)

INSIDE OUT

SPINNING FLAILS

A flail is a long chain that is spun around rapidly. In the past, farmers have used flails to clear vegetation. In World War I the British fitted flails to tanks. The heavy steel chains detonated mines buried beneath the ground. The tanks cleared safe paths for soldiers through minefields. A mine blast shakes the chains of the flail but does not destroy them.

ROTOR
spins with chains or chisels to blow up mines hidden in the ground.

2010 ›››

LONG-DISTANCE
A drone named Zephyr 7 flies for over 336 hours. It uses **solar power** for its journey.

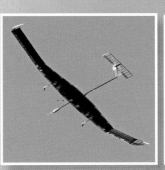

2011 ›››

DIGGER D-3
Swiss mine-clearance organizations begin to use the remote-controlled robotic vehicle Digger D-3 to clear mines.

hunter-killer—a device that can both locate targets and destroy them
solar power—energy generated from sunlight

URBAN DRONES

In Iraq British forces have been fighting terrorists who hide among local people. Much of the fighting takes place in towns and cities. Every time a patrol turns a corner, it might be exposed to attack.

The Black Hornet is a tiny drone. It is only a few inches across. Soldiers use it in urban warfare. The drone has a tiny camera. Using a tablet, the soldiers fly the drone around corners, above walls, or into buildings. They follow the drone's course on a screen, checking for enemy fighters or suspicious devices, such as bombs. This is far safer than the traditional method of patrolling. Soldiers carry two drones in a small pack on their belts. The pack contains batteries to charge the drones. While one drone is flying, the other is being charged.

THREE CAMERAS take detailed still and video images.

BATTERY beneath the drone is rechargeable.

TIMELINE

2011
DAKSH
The Indian Army introduces the Daksh bomb-disposal robot. It is radio controlled. Daksh uses a powerful jet of water to defuse bombs.

2013
BLACK HORNET
The British and Norwegian armies begin to use the Black Hornet Nano drone for urban fighting.

SPECIFICATIONS

BLACK HORNET NANO
Weight: 0.56 ounce (16 grams)
Length: 4 inches
(10.1 centimeters)
Top speed: 11 miles
(18 kilometers) per hour
Range: 1 mile (1.6 kilometers)

INSIDE OUT

URBAN WARFARE
Soldiers use Black Hornets in urban settings. The drones gather information about hidden dangers. They have three cameras. One points forward, one points straight down, and one points down at an angle of 45 degrees. The drones can also carry infrared devices that allow them to operate at nighttime.

ELECTRIC ROTORS
are designed to be as
quiet as possible.

2013 》》》

TARANIS
The British develop a long-distance drone called the Taranis. It uses **stealth** technology to avoid detection by radar.

2014 》》》

EAGLE DRONE
The MQ-1C Gray Eagle long-range endurance drone begins to replace the MQ-1 Predator in U.S. military service.

stealth—using advanced materials and design to make an object hard to detect by radar

CARRIER DRONES

The U.S. Navy has a program to develop its own drones. These UAVs need to be able to take off from and land on aircraft carriers. The Navy has investigated a number of drones.

One version of the new U.S. Navy drone was called Unmanned Carrier-Launched Airborne **Surveillance** and Strike (UCLASS). The X-47B used sensors and cameras to monitor activity on the ground. It also carried missiles and could refuel other aircraft in the air. After UCLASS had been built and tested, however, the Navy decided to develop the Carrier-Based Aerial-Refueling System (CBARS) instead. When it is completed, CBARS will allow crewed aircraft to fly longer missions without having to land.

ANGLED SURFACES do not reflect radio waves back to radar devices.

EXHAUST is on top of the aircraft, so it is less detectable by sensors on the ground.

TIMELINE

2015
NORTHROP X-47B
Having been tested on land in 2011, the X-47B has its first trials taking off and landing from aircraft carriers.

2015
MAARS
The U.S. Marines display the MAARS, an advanced armed robotic system. MAARS is armed with a machine gun and four grenade launchers.

SPECIFICATIONS

X-47B

Weight: 14,000 pounds
(6,350 kilograms)
Length: 38 feet 2 inches (11.63 meters)
Main armament: Up to 4,500 pounds
(2,000 kilograms) of bombs
Top speed: 685 miles
(1,102 kilometers) per hour
Range: 2,416 miles (3,889 kilometers)

INSIDE OUT

CARRIER DRONES

Drones used on aircraft carriers have different qualities from ordinary drones. A catapult fires them off the carrier, but landing is more difficult. It requires a highly sensitive system that responds to the movement of the carrier deck. Aircraft carriers have many radio-based systems, so drones have to be able to resist interference from radio waves. In addition, aircraft carriers only have limited storage space below decks. The X-47B has folding wings so it takes up less room.

FOLDING WINGS
allow easier storage on
aircraft carriers.

2016

URAN-6

Russia begins using the Uran-6, a tracked robot armed with four video cameras. Uran is designed to clear minefields safely.

2016

UCLASS

The U.S. Navy decides to develop a new aerial refueling drone in place of its UCLASS drones.

surveillance—the close observation of someone or something

NEW GENERATION

All branches of the U.S. military now have their own drones. Drones vary from tiny, hand-held devices to aircraft that are almost as large as passenger airliners.

Unmanned aerial vehicles such as the Avenger, also known as the Predator C, fly farther and carry heavier weapons than earlier drones. Their cameras and sensors are upgraded to show the smallest possible detail. In the past, drone warfare has been criticized. People say that drone strikes have killed innocent people by mistake. Military forces are eager to make sure that drones only hit targets whose identity is certain. Modern drones are all designed and built using stealth technology. This prevents them from appearing on enemy radar and being shot down.

LONG BODY
allows more room to carry bombs inside the aircraft.

INTO THE FUTURE

MAARS
The U.S. Marines are developing the Modular Advanced Armed Robotics System, or MAARS. These small robots carry machine guns and other weapons. They are designed to be positioned near **infantry** positions or Marine bases. They can detect movement and will automatically fire at any approaching enemy soldiers. Controllers use seven onboard cameras to follow and control the robot's movements.

SPECIFICATIONS

PREDATOR C AVENGER
Weight: 18,200 pounds
Length: 44 feet (13 meters)
Main armament: 6,500 pounds
  (2,900 kilograms) of missiles, rockets,
  and bombs
Top speed: 460 miles (740 kilometers)
  per hour
Flight range: 20 hours

IN ACTION

DRONE PILOTS

Drone operators are all trained pilots. They fly drones from air bases in the United States by following video links and maps. Pilots work with a team of air crew, who help navigate the aircraft, analyze video film and photographs, and identify targets. Pilots often say that flying a drone is like playing a video game. Unlike a video game, however, a drone strike has deadly consequences. Drone pilots have targeted and killed leading terrorist commanders in conflicts in Afghanistan and Iraq.

AIR INTAKE
on top of the drone sucks in air that is pushed through the engine.

SPECIAL WINGS
improve low-speed flying, so that the drone can land on aircraft carriers.

MQ-25 STINGRAY
The MQ-25 Stingray is the latest drone being developed by the U.S. Navy. It will be used mainly for mid-air refueling. However, it will also be equipped with hardpoints that will allow it to carry missiles and rockets.

infantry—soldiers who fight on foot

GLOSSARY

allies (AL-lyz)—a group or country that works together with other groups or countries to achieve a purpose

altitude (AL-tuh-tood)—height above sea level

bombardier (bom-buh-DEER)—the member of an airplane crew who aims and releases bombs

casualty (KAZH-oo-uhl-tee)—a person who is injured or killed in a war

combat engineer (COM-bat en-juh-NEER)—a soldier who performs demolitions or does construction work

fuse (FEWZ)—a timer that controls when a bomb explodes

Gatling cannon (GAT-ling CAN-nun)—a machine gun with a number of rotating barrels

hardpoint (HARD-poynt)—a place on an airplane designed to carry weapons

hunter-killer (HUN-tur KILL-uhr)—a device that can both locate targets and destroy them

improvise (IM-pruh-vize)—to create without special planning or equipment

infantry (IN-fun-tree)—soldiers who fight on foot

infrared (IN-frah-red)—an invisible form of energy, such as heat

insurgent (in-SUR-gent)—a person fighting against a government

parachute (PARE-uh-shoot)—a cloth canopy that slows down objects or people as they fall through the air

radar (RAY-dar)—a location device that works by bouncing radio waves off objects

reconnaissance (ree-KAHN-uh-sents)—military observation to find out information about the enemy

resistance (rih-ZISS-tuhns)—a secret organization resisting a foreign army

satellite (SA-tuh-lite)—communications based on devices in orbit in space around the Earth

sensor (SEN-sor)—a device that measures and responds to a quality such as heat

stealth (STELTH)—using advanced materials and design to make an object hard to detect by radar

solar power (SO-lur POW-ur)—energy generated from sunlight

surveillance (suhr-VAY-luhnss)—the close observation of someone or something

warhead (WAR-hed)—the part of a bomb or missile that carries explosives

READ MORE

Chandler, Matt. *Military Drones*. Drones. North Mankato, Minn: Capstone Press, 2017.

Clay, Kathryn. *Robots in Risky Jobs: On the Battlefield and Beyond*. The World of Robots. North Mankato, Minn: Capstone Press, 2014.

Faust, Daniel R. *Military Drones*. Drones: Eyes in the Skies. New York: PowerKids Press, 2016.

Spilsbury, Louis, and Richard Spilsbury. *Robots in the Military*. Amazing Robots. New York: Gareth Stevens Publishing, 2015.

INTERNET SITES

Use FactHound to find Internet sites related to this book.

Visit www.facthound.com

Just type in 9781515791997 and go.

Super-cool stuff!

Check out projects, games and lots more at
www.capstonekids.com

INDEX